D1607960

# SIX MONTHS
# AMONG INDIANS

**1983**

This edition typeset and reproduced from the original format handset in Darius Cook's newspaper office in Niles, Michigan, in 1889.

# SIX MONTHS AMONG INDIANS

by
DARIUS B. COOK

Published
By

Avery Color Studios
AuTrain, Michigan 49806

ISBN 0-932212-30-1


First Edition - February 1983

# SIX MONTHS AMONG INDIANS,
## WOLVES AND OTHER WILD ANIMALS,
### IN THE FORESTS OF ALLEGAN COUNTY, MICH.,
#### IN THE WINTER OF 1839 AND 1840.

---

## INTERESTING STORIES OF FOREST LIFE.

---

## THE EXPLOITS OF TECUMSEH AND OTHER CHIEFS, THEIR CRUELTY TO CAPTIVES

---

### HOW TECUMSEH WAS KILLED AND WHO KILLED HIM

---

### TRUE INDIAN STORIES OF THE WAR OF 1812-13.

## BY DARIUS B. COOK.

PRINTED AND PUBLISHED BY THE AUTHOR.
NILES MIRROR OFFICE, NILES, MICH.
1889.

# PREFACE

DARIUS B. COOK
1815—1901

The author of this work never contemplated its publication until within a short time. Glancing at his diaries and seeing many events which history does not contain, he deemed it a duty which every man owes to his fellow citizens and country to contribute all possible to past events, especially of the savage tribes who used to roam through our forests, and who are rapidly passing away and in a few years will only be known as handed down by the historians. No effort is made in any thing but a plain statement of occurrences which took place. The interviews happened to be with the older ones who were actually in the war of 1812 and fought with the British, and been themselves engaged in many bloody contests and taken many scalps. Without further preface we trust this book will be received as adding a little contribution to the history of the past.

DARIUS B. COOK

Niles, Mich., 1889.

TO
JAMES RHODES,
the faithful
and jolly companion, whose
heart beat for the welfare of the whole
human race, who was a steadfast friend, who
knew no fear, and was ever ready to sac-
rifice himself for one he admired—to
him, wherever he may be,
this little history is
respectfully
dedicated.

# AUTHOR

Darius B. Cook, 1815-1901, was a pioneer Michigan newspaperman. Beginning as a printer's devil in Litchfield, Connecticut, he later worked on Bennett's New York Herald, the Saturday Evening Post, Baltimore Sun and Richmond Enquirer. In Washington, while on the National Intelligencer, he listened to the Senate debates of Clay, Calhoun and Webster.

In 1836 he joined the migration to Michigan and moved between the Pontiac Courier, Kalamazoo Gazette and Detroit Free Press until 1842 when he loaded a big hand press on a wagon and started for Chicago. His journey ended along the way during an overnight stay in Niles where the townspeople, learning he was not only a journalist, but a Democratic journalist, persuaded him to stay. Active until his death nearly sixty years later, he edited and published the Niles Republican (he changed the paper's politics, but not its name), the Niles Globe and the Niles Mirror.

He was the first of four generations of Cook family newspapermen in Niles. His son Fred W., grandson Fred D., and great grandson Sheridan continued the tradition until the 1970's.

Darius Cook, as an editor, reflected Nineteenth Century Michigan: direct, colorful and political. His newspapers were lively and interesting, showing the mark of a man who recognized a good story... such as the one he wrote in SIX MONTHS AMONG IN-DIANS.

# INTRODUCTION

Darius Cook was a young newspaperman in Kalamazoo when one morning his doctor told him, "Go live with the Indians, sleep in their wigwams, live as they live, and the chances are you will recover." SIX MONTHS AMONG INDIANS is his account of how he and James Rhodes followed the doctor's advice.

During the winter of 1839-1840, they lived in an abandoned cabin in the Allegan County, Michigan wilderness trapping wolves, hunting deer, living the great adventure.

Forest life in 1839-1840 was not dull. Wolves circled the cabin nightly. Indians, and later a bear, ransacked it. Cook was treed by a wolf. He and Rhodes rescued the wife of an Indian chief from wolves. They witnessed a scalp dance; sat beside a fire listening to old Indians delight in recollections of American scalps taken in the War of 1812.

Two of the Indians...Noonday, chief of the Grand River Ottawas, and Sagemaw (Cook calls him Saginaw), a local Potowatomi chief...provided the material for several chapters including Noonday's firsthand reminiscence of Tecumseh's death in the Battle of the Thames.

The whole of SIX MONTHS AMONG INDIANS is a firsthand reminiscence...of a pioneer Michigan winter's biting cold, of the silences in the big woods, of the full game pole and snarling wolves beyond the firelight...as well as the story telling of the old Indians in their last days on old hunting grounds, all seen and heard, lived and recorded by a young newspaperman.

# TABLE OF CONTENTS

# CHAPTER I.

*A Winter in the Forests of Allegan County—1839 - 40.—Wolves, Indians and Game Plenty.*

It was the second week in November, 1839, when ill health caused the writer to abandon a pleasant yet laborious position in the office of the "Kalamazoo Gazette," published at Kalamazoo, Mich., Henry Gilbert, editor and proprietor, for a life with the Indians.

"How are you this morning?" said Dr. Starkweather, as he entered the office one morning and found us pale and coughing over the office. stove.

"No better, doctor; I passed a sleepless night, and you can see I am about ready to surrender."

"Not yet," said the doctor. "You want fresh air and exercise. Go live with the Indians, sleep in their wigwams on a bed of leaves, hunt in the forests, live as they live, and the chances are you will recover. Pure air, rarefied by the trees in the forest, will do any man good."

"Yes, but I could not endure such exposure."

"Go join the Rev. Mr. Selkirk, an Indian missionary near Allegan, and make your home in the wigwams, and you will be sure to live or die in six weeks. You cannot live and sleep in this office."

The doctor was in earnest. It seemed a great undertaking for a young man, but preparations were hurriedly made. A companion seemed necessary for such an expedition, and one was soon found fond of adventure, named James Rhodes. He was young, full of nerve, energy, life and courage. Eight large wolf traps, with spikes, which had to be set with levers, were procured, rifles and ammunition, a bed, blankets and necessary provisions, cooking utensils, etc., for a winter's campaign in the forests among the wolves and Indians.

The closing week in November, 1839, when every thing was in readiness, the two young men took leave of Mr. Gilbert, Volney Haskell, Orrin Case and all connected with the office, who gathered around us, laughing at our load, consisting of half of a dead horse for wolf bait, and a general outfit, on a sled, drawn by a yoke of oxen. We crossed the bridge spanning the Kalamazoo river, took the road to Gull Prairie, where we passed a night with Mr. and Mrs. Phinehas Cook, parents of the writer. Here our outfit was completed to perfection, and early in the morning we proceeded on our journey, passing our second night at Yankee Springs, a hotel kept by Yankee Lewis.

From Kalamazoo to Gull Prairie there were but two dwellings, and from the prairie to Yankee Springs but four, except the rude log houses erected by the Baptist missionary, Slater, for his Indian converts of the Ottawa tribe. Among them was Noonday, chief of the tribe, of whom we shall speak hereafter.

Mr. and Mrs. Lewis regretted exceedingly our rest would be disturbed by music and dancing, but such was our fate, for twenty couple kept the music going until daylight. The hotel was a good one for its day, and all travelers going to Grand Rapids made it a point to stop there. The writer can never forget the kind hearted Yankee Lewis and his estimable wife, who treated us so well, and sent us on our way with many kind wishes for our success.

Partaking of an early breakfast we pursued our journey for several miles, and ere we reached Rabbit river, turned on a blind road, lately blazed, to the north.

Companion Rhodes and the writer here left the sled and started ahead of the team on foot, that we might be more sure of following the road. The snow was getting deep, and deer tracks were abundant and fresh.

"I wish," said Rhodes, "I could got a crack at a big buck!" "So do I; we'd load him pretty soon." We were just rising a hill, and when we looked down from the summit, a big buck jumped up a little to our right not four rods off and stood broadside looking at us. Our rifles were on our shoulders and neither of us thought to shoot.

THE FIRST SHOT.

"Why don't you shoot?" said Rhodes. "Shoot yourself," said we. At this moment we both shot and wondered much to see him leap off. On close examination, his ball cut off a bush close to the ground within twenty feet of him, and ours went into a beech tree fifteen feet high, and the driver of the team had all the laugh to himself.

Onward we moved, on our winding way, until late in the afternoon we saw it lighter in the distance, and

> "We knew by the smoke which so gracefully curled
> "Above the green pines that a cottage was near."

A glistening diamond would not been half as welcome as that smoke, curling up in graceful folds amid the forest trees. There was a little opening and a rude log hut. It was the home of the first settler in that wilderness, Nelson Chambers. His nearest neighbor was a Mr. Barnes, about three miles, who had a saw mill at the head waters of Rabbit river. As we entered his clearing, both he and his solitary companion stood at their door gazing with wonder and amazement. They had never been visited by such a crowd. After explaining to them our mission, they extended the hand of welcome, such a welcome, too, as only pioneers know how to give to new comers. Such accommodations as they had were free, and we passed the night surrounded apparently with a hundred howling wolves who had got scent of our dead horse. We had now to proceed about three-fourths of a mile to an old log shingle shanty on land owned by a Mr. Seymour, of Allegan.

Early the next morning, Mr. Chambers piloted us to the place of destination, and there we unloaded our cargo. We found a hole in the ground, under an old pine bedstead, where we stored our potatoes to keep them free from frost, pegs in the logs to hang various articles upon. The hut was about twenty feet square. Many chinks between logs were out which we replaced. There was no chimney, but a place in one corner to build a log fire with a large opening above for the smoke. Our team left us soon after our first cold dinner in our new home was over.

THE OLD LOG CABIN.

The first work was to shovel the snow from the fireplace and prepare for a fire. The wolves had made this place their resort, as evinced by their tracks and hair and horns of deer which were seen in all directions. It was near sunset before preparations were completed for the night, and the wolves began their terrific music, which seemed to rend the air and caused us to look well to our fire during the long, cold and tedious night. Our horse flesh was placed on our cabin roof. Our provisions were stored inside. Sleep, there was little. The snuffing and growling of hungry wolves until daylight, no pen can describe.

> 'Twas if a thousand fiends of hell
> Were sending forth the battle yell.

# CHAPTER II.

*How to Catch Wolves—One on a Swing—A Visit from Adaniram.*

The sunshine in the morning was beautiful. The gentle breeze caused the stately pines to hum sweet music. The wolves had been hungry all the long night, howling here and there and amid the din the horned owl's tu-whit-tu-whoo! could be heard in all directions. Our breakfast consisted of baked potatoes, pork and pancakes, and nothing tasted more delicious. Notwithstanding the severe ordeal we had passed through, we already began to recover health and strength. The bait for wolves on the shanty came down and was dragged about three-fourths of a mile into a black ash swamp and left by a fallen tree. Three traps were set near it. To them a chain was attached and a heavy clog to the chain. Visiting the traps the next morning, two were gone and one was sprung, evidently by a piece of bark falling from the log. Not a vestige of the bait was left. Both were found. The clogs had caught against little trees, and the wolves had wound the chains around them and twisted their feet out, leaving the balls and claws in the traps.

We supplied bait the next night with the head of a deer and caught others, but they would twist out in the same manner. We found it was useless to catch them in this way, for so powerful were they no trap we had would hold them. We invented a plan to SAVE THEM.

A huge grape vine ran far up into the limbs of a tree, and both of us pulled it down and tied it to the roots of a tree with moose bark. We then cut it off and attached the chain of the trap to the vine, and the bait near the trap surrounding it in such manner that an animal must step over into the trap to get it. In this way we saved our first wolf. He was caught by the fore paw. He leaped and broke the bark, the vine sprung up and Mr. wolf was jerked two feet from the earth. At our appearance he could only kick at air and turn his head fiercely. Throwing a cord around the vine we could swing him thirty feet each way, and in this amusement we participated for some time, his feet touching the snow as he come down from his long sweep. A bullet through his head as he was sweeping up put an end to the sport.

Our custom after this was to bend down a sapling, tie it to the root of a tree and attach the chain to that. This would fly up and keep the wolf dancing upon his hind feet. In this way but one ever escaped, but, as will be seen hereafter, he was captured. Returning to our cabin early in the afternoon, we found it necessary to prepare huge logs to keep our fire going night and day. At this we spent two days.

In December a portion of the Pottawatomie tribe of Indians encamped a mile from us, east of Rabbit river, to hunt and trap, and prepare for making maple sugar in the spring. Among them was Adaniram Judson, an interpreter, a fine specimen of the tribe. He was educated by General Cass, and accompanied him in making treaties and to Washington. He was well versed in the English as well the Indian language. He possessed all the Indian traits and would not sleep in a bed. In his travels he would rest on the floor on a blanket, rather than a soft bed, being under the impression he would lose his elasticity and strength if he slept on anything soft. In our cabin his bed was a deer skin, with a wolf skin for a pillow. He gave us lessons in Indian, which we soon learned, finding it simple and easy. He was famed for his swiftness, and claimed he could run a mile on an Indian trail in four minutes. He prided himself on running down deer. Whenever he desired one, he took a track, followed it carefully until he started him, and then a steady trot, and in a short time would run one down and cut his throat. This has been done by many a young Indian buck. He was about 35 years old, medium heighth, and was one of the proudest Indians of the tribe, and claimed some of the blood of Saginaw, the old warrior chief. He was our frequent visitor while he remained in the forest, which was about six weeks. He would sing to us all the Indian songs, practice their dancing and war whoops, and make the wilderness echo far with his Indian yells. He was full of life and story.

On one occasion, retiring about midnight, he suddenly exclaimed, "Do you wish to hear the Indian story of the burning of Buffalo, in the war of 1812?"

"Oh, yes, Adaniram, we do."

Lifting himself up and resting on both elbows, he remarked, "Go with me to the wigwam of Saginaw to-morrow, take with you some fire water, get the chief a little drunk, and he will give you an unwritten history of the march there and the scenes at Buffalo.

It was about three miles to his wigwam on the trail. This was agreed to, and we all fell asleep amid the hooting of owls and howling of wolves.

ADANIRAM JUDSON.

# CHAPTER III.

*Visit to Saginaw—Scenes on the Way—Capture and Burning of Buffalo—Promise of the British— Women and Children Captives—The Fierce Blood of the Chief Boiling, etc.*

At break of day, Rhodes, who was a good cook, announced, "Breakfast is ready!" It consisted of coffee, roasted potatoes, venison and pancakes. This over, each with a rifle started on our tramp, Adaniram taking the lead. No trail was necessary for him; a glance at the trees told him his course, and we were not long in reaching the tent of the old chief. We found him sitting quietly in his wigwam, smoking a pipe which was once the property of Tecumseh, the brave. The pipe was presented to him by a British officer, for his skill and bravery in battle, the base of which was gold, mounted with pure silver. The stem was about 18 inches long, made with the quills of the wild turkey, supported by fine hickory splints, and wound with the sinews of deer. After his death, Saginaw, a chief and a great warrior, who was with Tecumseh when he fell, took his pipe, and it was his constant companion until his death. The writer saw it in the wigwam of Saginaw, and gave a pound of tobacco to the old chief for a smoke in it. It is undoubtedly still in existence among the tribe.

After the usual salutations, we were presented

to the scarred chief, who arose, extended his hand and received us with all the formalities which chiefs possess. We were seated upon bear skins which he had killed, the skulls of which were exhibited on poles which surrounded his wigwam. Saginaw was the first and only bald-headed Indian we had ever seen or heard of. There was a little hair on the back part of his head and extended from ear to ear. His furrowed brow, his wrinkled face and trembling hand placed him at about 80 years of age. He stood

SAGINAW.

six feet high and as straight as the arrows in his wigwam, and he walked with youthful elasticity. Many questions were asked relative to his life and his battles, but he would only answer with a "Ugh!" Finally we exclaimed, "Saginaw he buck-a-taw (want) whiskey?" "On-in-ta" (yes). Pulling out a small flask, he exclaimed, "ne-shin-che-mo-ke-mon!" (good whiteman). Turning a little into a bear's skull he drank it with a relish and called for more. A little more was given, and he soon began to sing and dance. Adaniram saw he was all right and he began to question him in Indian tongue and interpret as he proceeded. He had been in many a fight. He was with the British at the battle of the Thames, saw Tecumseh fall by a shot from a pistol drawn

DEATH OF TECUMSEH (BATTLE OF THE THAMES).

from a saddle by an officer whose horse had fallen over a log. He assisted Noonday in carrying his dead body from the field. He was not scalped as reported in some history. His blood was upon his

28

garments. He was carried far back in the retreat into his tent, and a great pow-wow was held over his dead body. After his fall, the Indians felt like fighting more. "Tecumseh kin-a-poo! Tecumseh kin-a-poo!" (Tecumseh is killed) sounded all along the line. The tomahawk of Tecumseh fell into the hands of Noonday; his pipe was secured by Saginaw; his war cap was torn to pieces in a strife among the tribe for it.

He gave a description of the march through Canada; how they climbed trees and shot American scouts. He said British officers had promised them all the women and children they could get if they would capture Buffalo, and they did as they promised to a great extent, and they had over one hundred women and children surrounded ready for torture. The women were separated from the children by a file of Indians, cruel, and thirsting for the order for torture. The work of throwing children into the burning buildings commenced. Saginaw would

THROWING CHILDREN INTO THE FLAMES.

take the feet and Sunagun the hands and swing—swing—swing, and over they went into the flames, and to see them writhe and die was glory enough for them. As he described the scene—the screaming and agony of women and mothers—he leaped high and gave the terrific war whoop and Indian yell at Buffalo, and exhibited all the ferocity he possessed at that time. He rushed to his *muhkuk* (a box made of bark), seized his scalping knife, and such demonstrations did he make with his hatchet and scalping knife that we stepped outside and cocked our rifles. Adaniram could not restrain him, and his three squaws rushed in, seized him and forced him to a seat on his bear skins.

The children were all to be thrown into the flames, and the women were to be led away captives, to be disposed of and tortured at their pleasure. Three had been thrown in when two British officers rode up, with drawn swords and ordered a halt, just in time to save a fourth. In a few moments a regiment of British regulars marched in and rescued the women and children. This exasperated the Indians to the highest pitch, and in the heighth of their indignation an arrow flew from the ranks and pierced the sword arm of one of the officers. It was a critical moment. Saginaw saw there was no such thing as restraining his braves (he did not wish to) and they were upon the point of dashing through the ranks and murdering and scalping the women and children when a number of British cavalry came dashing in among them and Saginaw commanded a halt. This undoubtedly saved the women and children, and a conflict with the regulars.

An Indian council was at once called. Sunagun said, "me no more fight for the British; me go to the Americans." Saginaw said, "me do so too." Noon-

INDIAN COUNCIL AT BUFFALO.

day said, "me go to mine wigwam." Several exciting speeches were made, when a number of the British cavalry rode in with pipes, tobacco, beads and Indian trinkets of all descriptions, and after a long parley it was agreed the matter should end and they smoked the pipe of peace.

# CHAPTER IV.

*Saginaw's Cruelty—His Smuggling Away of a Woman and a Girl—The Woman a Target for Young Bucks—The Girl raised with great care and Marries Saginaw's Son and has Children.*

CAPTURE OF ALICE AND EFFIE.

Saginaw was a brave and famous warrior, but like all his race, was cruel and delighted in torture. At Buffalo he smuggled away one woman, Alice, and a girl, Effie, the latter being about 12 years of age, beautiful black hair and eyes, round features, and cheeks as "rosy as the moon." The woman was used for a target for the young bucks to practice on.

They would stretch her arms out and tie each to a tree, pinion her feet and stand off a short distance and shoot at an arm, a finger, the breast, ear, a moccasin on top of her head, with blunt arrows, and she was bruised in a most shocking manner. One eye

YOUNG BUCKS PRACTICING.

was accidentally shot out and she suffered greatly, but only to the delight of her tormentors. At last the other eye was shot out and she was then pierced with arrows and left in the forest to be devoured by wolves.

The young girl, Effie, was watched with great care. The squaws became jealous of her and would have killed her had it not been for Saginaw who kept her guarded for a long time. She finally married one of Saginaw's sons and had five children and died at child-birth and there was great mourning at the time of her death.

The effects of fire-water passing off to a great extent, Saginaw sit down on his bear skin robe, his squaws, three in number, beside him, and all sang a song of peace and joy. As we were about to take our leave, he springs up and demands more fire-water. Adaniram grasps him, causing him to pause, while his squaws seize him and he surrenders, exclaiming "caw-in-ne-shin che-mo-ke-men!" (you are very bad white men.) Determined not leave him in a rage, a long parley ensued. We supplied him with tobacco and he mellowed down into pleasant songs. His squaws prepared a feast and we all partook heartily of muskrat soup served in bear skulls with wooden spoons. It was our first taste of that kind of soup, but it was well seasoned, mixed with pounded corn and very palatable.

The old chief became very loving ere we departed, about 2 p.m. and presented each of us with a pair of elegant moccasins which were tanned by his daughters, beaded and interwoven with porcupine quills with great taste.

On our return to what we called "hunters lodge," a strange animal was discovered at a distance in the crotch of a tree. We paused for a critical examination. We were scarcely within shooting distance and crept carefully along from tree to tree to get within range of our rifles. Both were to fire at the word, the same moment. No sooner had we got position than the animal leaped from one tree to another and then to the ground and flew swiftly away. What it was we could not determine.

During our absence some person had stolen the last ham from our lodge, and from the track, one being longer than another, owing to a deformity, we knew it was Indian Su-na-gun, but it was too late for pursuit that day. While discussing our supper, potatoes and pork, we heard what we supposed was the screaming of a woman, about half a mile distant, in great agony. It was fearfully dark and the wind whistled through the pines and the snow was falling fast. The wolves and the owls were hushed. This awful screaming of a woman in agony aroused our sympathies. No time was to be lost, and we left our supper and lit our torches, shouldered our rifles and were off with a rush. Onward we dashed in direction of the sound, but still we seemed to get no nearer to it, in fact it seemed farther and farther off, and we returned by our nearest neighbor, Mr. Chambers, who was listening to the same screams. On learning of our expedition, he laughed heartily and informed us it was a panther, and it had been in that vicinity several weeks. He had seen him twice. "Ah," says Rhodes, "that is what we were trying to get a shot at to-day, but he leaped from tree to tree, and then to the ground and dashed away."

"Yes, yes," says Chambers, "that was him; he is almost red, and is a large and powerful one." "But," says we, "it is dangerous to be in the forests, is it not, where they are?" "No," said Chambers, "they flee before a man, but I think it lucky you did not get a shot. If you had wounded him he would undoubtedly have made for you. Last spring there were two here, but the Indians killed one, and this one comes around occasionally perhaps to look up his mate." "Just so. Come Rhodes, let us to our lodge." The sound was finally lost in the distance, and the music of the wolves and owls was heard again. As we neared our lodge a little to the right two golden spots were seen glaring at our brilliant torch lights.

"Take this torch," said Rhodes, and the next

moment whang went his rifle and down fell a big buck with a bullet in his head.

"What shall we do with him?" was the next question. Leave him half an hour and the wolves would have him. To drag him to the lodge forty rods in the snow was a hard job for two already worn out. But there was no time lost; our torches were getting low and we had but one in reserve. "Let us try it," says Rhodes, strapping his rifle on his back and seizing one horn, and we the other. It was a two hundred pound buck or more, but we got him into camp and packed him away for the night. It was now ten o'clock, and, finishing our supper, we were in the hands of morpheus until broad day light.

# CHAPTER V.

*Wolves Stole our Pork—Bringing an Indian Thief to Confession.*

It fell to our lot to stir up the huge log fire in the corner and get the breakfast. Passing out to our pine dug out for pork, what was our surprise to find the wolves had pawed off the shingle blocks which covered it and taken every piece of pork—a two hundred log. They had followed the trail of the deer up to the door, making no noise, and robbed us of what we had outside. Here was the buck and we still had meat, and off came the hide, and in a few moments we were roasting pieces on sticks, Indian fashion, and made out our usual breakfast. The quarters were stuck upon poles outside; the balance carried to the marsh for wolves.

One event seemed to follow another in quick succession. On going to the spring about three rods distant, Su-na-gun was discovered coming on his trail to his hunting ground, when we dropped our pail and rushed back, seized our rifle, dashed out and exclaimed "nene kin-a-poo Su-na-gun!" (that is I will kill you.) He dodged behind a tree, but Rhodes made a dash for his rear and caused him to fall upon his knees and cry for mercy. We ordered him into our lodge with his rifle breech first, and he quickly obeyed. We pointed out to him where the ham hung and took away the bark we had placed to cover his track, and demanded he place his foot in it. This he declined to do and Rhodes cocked his rifle and he promptly obeyed; it was the short foot and a perfect fit. He owned up that he was the thief and begged for time to go to Yankee Springs for another. This was granted, and the next evening he came with one on his pony. This settled all stealing from that quarter and made them friends through fear. After this they thought we possessed great power and could tell who of them did wrong and they were more kind to us.

This over, we went to the swamp with the remains of the buck and found a monster wolf dancing on his hind legs, being jerked up by a spring pole. A wolf when trapped, can play well the penitent and sneak, but their teeth cut like plates of steel. We cast lots to see who should put a bullet through his head and it fell to Rhodes and he was not long in doing it. He was a monster. His carcass was dragged far away from the traps and placed in the crotch of a tree, for it was believed by Indians that wolves would never go near a dead one.

This over, we spent the balance of that day in preparing wood and for a trip each way, one up and one down the river, for our traps extended over three miles each way. The writer had a brother, Daniel, attending Barnes' mill, about three miles up the river whose estimable wife, Maria, always favored us with a loaf of bread.

# CHAPTER VI.

*Sport with Owls—A Wolf Trapped—Two Shot—*
*A call from Pe-make-wan, a Brother of Adaniram—*
*A Good Day's Work.*

It was a clear, cold morning in December. Breakfast was over; the huge log fire was burning briskly as we sat smoking our pipes and discussing whether we would go to our distant traps or stay around our cabin. The owls during the night had disturbed us exceedingly. It seemed as if all in the forest had gatherd with the wolves to give us one grand serenade. They were attracted by the venison which hung upon poles outside. In fact the owls had feasted upon it during the night, and the tracks of wolves were numerous around the lodge. We finally resolved to make war upon the owls and for two hours only. Both could imitate them to perfection. We started out in opposite directions and for some time we could shoot them without calling, being very numerous. When the call began they came from all directions. As fast as we could load and fire they would fall. We were not over eighty rods apart, judging from rifle reports, and we were striving to see who would bring in the greatest number. We met promptly on time, Rhodes having twenty-two to our eighteen. He could beat us in loading and firing.

It was exceedingly cold and we concluded to spend the day and pick off the thick matted feathers from the birds, make each a pillow, for as yet our cases were only stuffed with fine hemlock boughs. There seemed to be over two bushels of them, but on drying them a few days there were not enough for two pillows but by mixing them with the boughs they were all any one could desire.

At noon our picking was finished and our appetites were appeased by our usual home dinner. Our dishes were washed according to our custom by turning them bottom side up. We had just shouldered our rifles to visit our wolf traps when in came Pe-make-wan. He loosened his belt giving us to understand he was very hungry. We had plenty of cooked venison and cold roasted potatoes left and he cleaned it out in quick time and started with us for the traps. The snow was over a foot in depth. When we reached there we found one wolf dancing on the end of a pole, caught by the fore paw. He was soon dispatched, the trap re-set and our owls were left for bait. The wolf was left in a tree and we proceeded to a few traps on the bank of the river, about thirty-five rods distant. Reaching the river, brush were heard to crack on the opposite side. "Ke-wob-em," exclaimed Pe-make-wan, that is "you see?" In a moment a deer leaped into the river almost opposite us, and dashed up the bank not more than thirty yards from us. "Hold! hold!!" said Rhodes, don't shoot the deer!" No sooner had he spoken than two immense timber wolves dashed into the stream in the same place and were

40

quickly over. As they showed their heads above the bank, one of them fell by the deadly aim of Rhodes' rifle. The other received a bullet from our rifle, but made a leap for us. The second leap his back broke in the centre, the bullet cutting it half in two. The Indian discharged his rifle, cutting through the ear close into the head. With a broken back he struggled desperately for us. A bullet in his head from our revolver, put an end to him before a rifle could be loaded. These were soon skinned and their carcasses thrown into the river. On reaching our cabin, near evening, we found our only neighbor, Mr. Chambers, there with a supper all ready, roast venison, etc., with delicious wheat bread, which Mrs. C. frequently furnished, and perhaps we four did not enjoy a hearty meal and a pleasant evening. Mr. Chambers left for his home about 9 o'clock, but soon returned for a torch to protect himself from wolves.

# CHAPTER VII.

*How Wolves seek their Prey—The Rifle Failed us—*
*A Fierce Attack looked for—Piece of Hide, etc.*

The writer went to the spring at early dawn and discovered, near it, a solitary wolf track, fresh, in a light snow which had fallen during the night. It was agreed we would pursue that track after breakfast, especially as it went the course we desired to go to the river, Rhodes to go to the traps below, the writer above and beyond Barnes' mill. We had not followed over thirty rods when this single track branched into seven on a run. We concluded we had started a pack of wolves and it was useless to pursue, but we soon discovered they had started a deer. Three went to the right, three to the left and one followed on the track of the deer. Hunters understand that a deer, when startled, will leap off perhaps twenty rods and stop and look behind them. Rhodes took the tracks of those to the right, we to the left. He soon called to us to come. He stood where they had grabbed their game and drawn blood, but by a wonderful leap over a fallen tree top had escaped only to be caught by the three on the left and nothing was left but blood and hair. In numerous instances the same discoveries were made, which insured a hungry pack of wolves a feast, and they were far more destructive to deer than hunters.

Reaching the river, it was agreed we should

both be at the lodge at dusk. It was an established rule that the one who reached there first should fire a signal gun to be answered by the one in the forest. This was to be repeated every few minutes until ten o'clock in the evening. A shot by one out after dark was a signal to depart for him with a torch.

Thus we parted in opposite directions. Our small traps, which had not been visited for three days, contained muskrat and mink and ere we had gone a mile, an otter, and we found it necessary to pause and take off the hides. This detained us so we could not go the rounds and reach the lodge that evening, and were compelled to spend the night with a Mr. Hooker, residing near Barnes' mill, who moved there from Gull Prairie, Kalamazoo county. Here we were beyond the sound of the signal gun. We made our supper out of cold roasted potatoes and dried venison we had carried in our pocket. His was a log cabin with a stick chimney on the outside. A terrible wind storm, accompanied with a light snow continued all night, and the thermometer must have been below zero, yet the snow melted and the roof leaked in various places. Our coffee in the morning was made of hemlock boughs and was excellent. Mr. Hooker was poor but hospitable and gave us the best he had, well cooked corn coon and pancakes.

Breakfast over, our journey up the river was not yet completed. The wind was blowing powerfully, but we pushed along steadily on our trail and came to a thicket of hazel bushes. Here rabbits had been playing very thick and we concluded we would have one for Mr. Hooker on our return. Glancing cautiously in every direction to get a shot at one, to our surprise, we saw a

MONSTROUS GRAY WOLF,

43

not three rods distant, hunting for rabbits. Directly in our front was a large log which we used for a trail through the thicket and upon this the wolf placed his fore paws, and was smelling for something on the other side. He was a monster. The big ruffle on his throat told us he was an old settler. Placing our rifle by a large tree where we stood, we took deliberate aim back of his chops to sever the artery. The cap burst, but the rifle failed to go off. Quick as thought, the wolf came directly at us with wonderful ferocity. In a moment we drew our huge hunting knife from our belt and as he came down by the tree we made a desperate plunge at him, taking completely out of his back a piece of hide as large as the palm of the hand. The wolf made a square angle and swept through the hazel brush from us at the top of his speed, followed by a shot from our revolver. The tree hid us from his view, and he was frightened by the explosion of the cap, the wind blowing powerfully, he ran accidentally toward us. It was a trying moment. He was a powerful animal terrible in battle, and it was a plunge for life. One closing of his jaws would have crushed a bone instantly, but with our knife we felt quite sure of victory. Retracing our steps to Mr. Hooker's, we found the water from the roof had dripped into our rifle during the night and wet the powder.

Before completing our journey up the river we began to think of our companion who expected us back, as agreed, and we hastened our speed homeward on our back track. Coming within sight of where we had skinned our game we saw Rhodes examining closely for our rifle in the snow, or clothing, for there was plenty of blood and a pack of

44

wolves had evidently quarreled for the carcasses. We hailed him at a distance and he threw his hunting cap high. It was a happy meeting. Our furs testified our excuse for not returning.

Turning our course toward the Indian encampment, the first one we met was Gosa, whose niece had disgraced him, and over which he and his squaw mourned, for virtue among the tribe was a treasure. A step outside was disgraceful and was only settled by marriage or large gifts. Entering his wigwam, he pointed out to us his niece and the shame which was strapped to her back. All squaws bore their papooses on their backs and all had to do all the hard labor, prepare all the wood, dress all the game, tan the hides, while the Indians hunt and bring in the game. His niece, Lydia, was subject to terrible abuse and she appealed to us for protection. We called Gosa from his wigwam and told him the great spirit would not let him go to the happy hunting grounds when he died if he did not cease such punishment and treat her lovingly. No one can tell the joy of that erring girl when he pledged us he would cease his punishments. She wept and threw herself at our feet expressing, in Indian dialect, great gratitude. Scars from whips, made from sinews of deer, were all over her person. He claimed he hated to do it, but it was the command of the great spirit. We soon pursuaded him that such laws were condemned by white men and the great spirit.

Lydia was so well pleased that she brought us muskrat to eat and gave each a pair of moccasins. Her uncle had never had such teachings and there was nothing too good for us. He afterwards would drive deer to us on their runway and gave us the use of his ponies.  Arriving at the lodge near sunset, we found every thing had been stolen.  Not a potato or a particle of any thing eatable, except the venison on the poles, was left, and that made our supper.

# CHAPTER VIII.

*The Pursuit—The Surrender—The Trick on Rhodes
—More Indians—A Settlement and Feast.*

At Early dawn we took the trail and moved as rapidly as the deep snow would permit. We were armed with our rifles, our revolvers and hunting knives. We tramped over four miles before we discovered the smoke of their wigwams and we paused to rest and form plans for a surprise.

Rhodes was a short, thick set young man, with long dark brown hair, heavy whiskers all over his face, hazel eyes piercing from beneath shaggy brows, and dressed in his hunting garb and armed, he looked like a wild devil let loose in the forest. His tiger was up, for it was the second time we had been robbed and it would not hurt his conscience to shoot an Indian now any more than it would a wolf. He could talk the language better than the writer and he was chosen to do it.

All arranged, we dashed in upon them, but were seen by many, who rushed to their wigwams. They knew our mission well and skulked from our view. Rhodes called for the chief among them and he came out; he then demanded the surrender of the thieves. (It was a new band, one we had never seen and did not know of their arrival.) The chief was a young, fierce buck, slender, and seemed anxious to assist us, but evidently was not. He went with us from one wigwam to another and we found a blanket and a piece of deer skin which we recognized. Rhodes seized the blanket and demanded a surrender of all they possessed and assured them he had a band who would march in upon them. He commanded one and another to stand up and they promptly obeyed. The young chief, or the leader of the band, ordered that all engaged in the robbery, to come forth. They did so and there were seven, and the measures in our game sacks of their feet told truly of four of them. They claimed we were not settlers, but intruders upon their hunting and trapping grounds, but they wanted no war; they would do any thing to settle it. Rhodes, mellowing down, said he, too, desired peace. He came in there to join them, to live with them. He loved the good Indian and would defend them. At least thirty Indians, squaws and children gathered around. The squaws brought out some of our ham and the otter, deer and wolf skins they had stolen. One of the turbulent ones, on seeing this cried out, "Caw-in-ne-shin squaw!" meaning you are a very mean squaw. He was silenced by the young chief, but he could hardly restrain his rage. We took out a pencil and a memorandum book and asked his name with a view to take him to Allegan for punishment. This immediately brought him to terms and he gave his name as San-go-far. It was finally agreed that the party should return what they had left of the stolen goods and go to Yankee Springs and bring in more. Early the next morning four of them appeared on their ponies, loaded with furs of all varieties and deposited them on our bed. This was to show their sincerity, but it increased our cares,for it was well known we daily left our lodge alone, without any way to prevent the entrance of any one. If the door was barred it was an easy matter to climb up on the logs outside and down them inside, and it was suspected a portion of the band might skulk around and when we left, enter and take the furs and charge us with the theft. We therefore cast lots to see who should remain in the lodge that day. It fell to Capt. Rhodes, as we afterwards called him, to remain and for us to go to the wolf traps. It was an exceedingly hard punishment for him to be thus confined, but he endured it, spending some of his time in preparing "jerked venison."

On nearing our wolf traps we saw the back of an immense animal curve up behind the large log where one was set. We paused for a survey. Moving cautiously around the butt of the log we were discovered and the monster made a fearful leap for us, but he was fast in the trap, the chain of which was attached to a small tree, and although he struggled with great power to reach us he could not. A bullet finished him in few seconds. What it was we could not tell. Its large, round head and paws, sharp and immense claws showed it was of the cat species. It proved to be a large lynx. We strung him up to a tree while we proceeded to our other traps down the river but found little of importance. Returning, a solitary wolf had been attracted by the blood, but passed on. It was a hard drag through the snow to the lodge, but we reached there about 4 p.m. and found the Captain in a profound sleep, such as weary hunters enjoy. We quietly slipped off the furs and secreted them outside in the dug out. Still, he was in a deep sleep with his rifle by his side. This, too, was secreted. The lynx was then carefully placed by his side. We climbed upon the roof where we could look down unseen. It was a sight never to be forgotten. His face was towards the logs and at his back lay the monster animal. Fearing he might sleep until sundown we set up an Indian yell that aroused him. He grabbed for his rifle and struck against the lynx. He leaped up in an instant, looked for his rifle, but contented himself with his revolvers. He satisfied himself the animal was dead and he rolled him off the bed. The furs and his rifle were gone. Some one had stolen them during his sleep and he went searching for a trail. While doing this we slipped down inside the cabin. It was some time before he returned and found us preparing supper. We questioned him closely relative to what had been going on. He admitted having fallen asleep, that the furs and rifle were stolen. He could give no information relative to the mysterious appearance of the animal, but "it must have been the work of Indians." On searching, every thing was soon found and he was forcibly reminded that he was a very careless watchman.

We were sipping tea, borrowed from Chambers, when we heard the Indians coming with a yell which drowned the voice of old wolf, Jim, as we called him, who always howled at late twilight and was answered by numerous wolves in various places. They rode up to our door and dismounted, bringing in provisions, tobacco, pipes, far more than they had stolen. We were prepared for them as much as possible. Mrs. Chambers had supplied us with bread. Rabbits and venison were in readiness on a table made of split pine, supported by shingle blocks. Their ponies were turned loose, but would scarcely leave the tree tops near us. There was a jolly time at this feast. San-go-far was the principal talker. He was full of story of his adventures and often would express his sorrow at what he had done to us. But it was all settled and we all sat before the blazing logs smoking the pipe of peace until midnight, when all fell asleep with their furs around them. A yell in the morning brought up their ponies and they left before breakfast. One hearty meal will answer an Indian two or three days. When he eats he lets loose his belt and fills himself as much as possible, and as he grows hungry he tightens it.

# CHAPTER IX.

*Visit to Selkirk Mission—Pursued by Wolves on our Return and Treed—The Rescue.*

Opening the door in the morning, a fine buck stood about ten rods distant , browsing from a tree top lately fallen. He was facing us. "Now," says the Captain, "strike the curl in front." It was a splendid mark, and not an Indian in the forest could beat either of us. Standing inside the door we made the shot and the deer fell in his tracks with an exact centre shot. Really, there was no object in killing one for their meat was worth nothing to us and only two cents a pound in any of the villages and it cost all it was worth to get it there. We got the Indians to tan the hides.

"Captain, I am going to the Selkirk mission today," said we; "will be back in due season this evening." An Indian pilot had tarried with us over night and off we started. It was seven or eight miles; we struck a trail in about a mile. We reached the mission about 11 a.m. and were received by the Reverend with the greatest hospitality.

This Mr. Selkirk was a former, and we believe, the first Episcopal Minister stationed at Niles, Mich. He had in his charge about one hundred and forty Indians, old and young, whom he was educating and they seemed in a prosperous condition. He treated us to a sumptuous dinner and two hours were spent pleasantly. A number of the young men in his charge, as well as the old, took great interest, and it was his delight to teach them

We left for our lodge about 2 p.m., leaving our guide at the mission. We had no trouble in following our trail back until within a mile of camp when another track interfered and for some distance followed ours. When we arrived to where ours was first struck it was hard to tell which led to our lodge. By this we were led off and darkness began to cast a deep shadow and old Jim began to howl. The signal gun was fired, answered by ours. It was getting dark and we began to think of a fire. Another gun convinced us that the Captain was coming to our rescue. Gun answered gun as the wolves gathered around. In the deep snow our progress was slow. We heard the growl of a wolf in our rear. It was dark and gloomy. We grasped the limb of a small beech tree and leaped into its branches and not too soon, for a big wolf was near us. We let off our rifle as near as possible in the darkness at the wolf, which was answered by the Captain with a yell not forty rods off. Soon a light was seen in the distance and as it drew near, hurrah answered hurrah with great cheer. During this time wolves were all around but could not be seen. On the appearance of the torches they fled, always fearing a fire in the night. This endeared the Captain to us more than ever, but he did nothing more than had been done to him on a previous occasion on a bitter cold night when he was treed by them half a mile out. There was not a night the wolves did not follow us to our lodge as seen by their tracks in the morning.

At early dawn a little son of Mr. Chambers came

to our lodge for us to come at once to his house and
we did so. We mistrusted what he wanted for he had
a wolf pen built of logs a few rods from his house.
It was about fifteen feet square; the top sloped so an
animal could walk up to a hole in the centre, under
and inside of which was a dead carcass. Two wolves
had jumped in and once in they could not get out.
Here they were, one a monster, the other medium
size. Occasionally they would make a desperate
leap for the hole above and strike their fore paws
against the logs and drop back. We stirred them up
with poles which they would break in a moment.

After amusing ourselves with driving them around
the pen as long as we desired, Mr. Chambers took
our rifles and dispatched them. This was in February, the month when deer congregate, and on our

return to the lodge not less than thirty were seen in a drove. It was a beautiful sight, so many deer, with their white flags up, dashing through the forest. The Captain gave one of them a shot and brought him down and gave him to our benevolent friend, Mr. Chambers.

Nothing of interest occurred for several days, and we had jolly times with the Indians, shooting at marks with rifles and arrows. It was great sport for the young bucks to shoot and beat us with arrows. They would hit a cent fifty feet away nearly every shot. They finally brought out a young squaw who could beat all of them. She never sighted over the arrow, but would fix her eye on the mark and let the arrow fly without a miss.

The Indian way of making maple sugar is to cut into the tree with a hatchet and drive a sheet iron spout into the tree under the hack. The sap was caught in wooden troughs. They would boil muskrat, coon, dog, or whatever they wished to eat in it. When boiled down to syrup they would strain it through deer's hair, then make it into sugar and sell it to the whites. Straining it through hair would make the syrup look quite clear and improve the appearance of the sugar very much. Gosa made large quantities of it.

# CHAPTER X.

*A Squaw up a Tree—Her Screams are Heard—The Rescue—A Hard Time—It Proves to be one of Saginaw's Wives—Great Rejoicing—A Feast.*

It was a still, cold night, the moon and the stars shone bright, all nature was hushed and naught but the wolves and owls seemed to disturb the solemn silence; yet, sounds from afar seemed to echo through the forest as we went out to roll in a log to replenish our fire. "Hark!" said the Captain, as we tipped the log up on the end and were about to drop it into the cabin, "what sound is that?" "It is the same old panther, far away," said I, and down went the log and we rolled it on the fire.

It was our turn to prepare supper and the kettle was on the coals, the venison was on sticks before the fire, the potatoes were in the ashes. He steps out to listen and returns saying—"it does not sound like a panther; it seems, too, in the same place all the time." Again I listen—"No—hark again!" It is a terrible moan, far distant, and amid howling wolves. We lost no time in preparing for as hasty a pace as possible. Our rifles were in order, our torches were ablaze. Through the deep snow we made our way, not with a swift and tiresome tread, but slow and steady gait. Nearer and nearer each step brought us to the dismal sound. First one would take the lead to break the path then the other. When within about twenty rods, we paused to get a distinct sound. It was indescribable, a hoarse, mournful, deep, guttural sound, like one in the last agonies of despair, amid devouring wolves.

THE RESCUE.

"Hold my torch," said the Captain, "while I strap my rifle to my back." It was but the work of a moment. "Give me your torch and step forward with rifle cocked," said he, "and I, with a torch in each hand, will follow close behind. Look sharp for glaring eyes and we'll move swiftly to the spot."

Soon as the light penetrated to the place, the shouts of a squaw were heard, but faintly. We then shouted in Indian language at the top of our voices "we are coming! we are coming!!" The wolves fled from before our blazing torches, and she cried out, meaning "I am saved!" and faintly expressed great gratitude.

She was about twelve feet high upon the limb of a beech tree, cold and stiff, scarcely able to help herself. "Quick! quick!! take our rifle," and I was at her side in a moment, but not being able to untie the buckskin belt which bound her to the tree, we took cords from our pocket, placed them under her arms, threw them over a limb, cut the belt and let her safely down. She could scarcely move, except her arms. Strapping our rifles on our backs, each with his torch in hand, she threw an arm around each neck and we started for the lodge, her feet dragging in the snow. It was a terrible task. Her limbs were so benumbed with cold she could scarcely move them and we sometimes carried her a few rods. Fatigued with the toils of the day we were not well nerved for this task. The wolves were in close pursuit and not infrequently did we pause and shoot at their glaring eyes, reflected by the light. The more we compelled her to move her limbs the easier it was. After the first half mile she was able to render some assistance, which was a great relief. Although she would not weigh over one hundred and twenty-five pounds, it seemed three hundred.

At last we reached the lodge and laid her down in front of the fire on deer skins and covered with the same wolf skins. She seemed now almost insensible. A sack of hot ashes was placed at her feet, hot stimulants administered. Every thing was done to restore her possible. Circulation returning, she fell into a deep sleep from which she did not awake

fell into a deep sleep from which she did not awake until eight o'clock in the morning. Our venison and potatoes, which we left by the fire was burnt up and we went supperless to bed.

When she awoke, venison, potatoes and coffee was ready and she partook with great relish. Her first utterance was an expression of gratitude to us for her deliverance from a terrible death. She then informed us how she came there. She went the day before to the Selkirk mission to visit her sister. There she remained over night and left in the afternoon later than she supposed. Her sister accompanied her some distance and returned. Before she was aware of it night was upon her and wolves on her track. She knew well her doom. She knew both of us well and knew if she could get within hearing distance she might be rescued. She ran until she knew wolves were close upon her and leaped into the tree where we found her. Both of us had seen her but she would not tell us who she was. She was medium height, rather slim, fine features, with hair and eyes black as the raven. One of her toes was a little frozen.

Breakfast being over we proposed to accompany her to her wigwam. This she begged us not to do. She took her departure with tears in her eyes, thanking us over and over for the kindness she had received. We had determined to rest that day.

Early the next morning a young buck, dressed in rich Indian costume, with a rod in his hand, came dashing up to our door on a beautiful pony, and hailing us exclaimed, in Indian, "Saginaw wishes to see both of you early!" and without further explanation wheeled his pony and galloped away.

"Great heavens!" exclaimed the Captain, "that was one of Saginaw's wives!" "That's so," said I, and the old villain has killed two Indians through jealousy!"

"I do not care to go today," said the Captain. "Wait a day or so until he cools off." After discussing the matter for some time, "I'm going," said he. "So am I," was the response, but go prepared for the worst, and if there is any demonstration we'll fix him."

Our hunting garbs were on in a moment. Our revolvers were in our belts loaded. We were both young, swift and enduring, and been long enough in the forest to know no fear. We moved rapidly and it was not long before we saw the smoke of his wigwam and paused to look well to our rifles. When within a short distance the squaw we had rescued came out to meet us and said "Saginaw was good Indian now." We uncocked our rifles and were escorted to his wigwam. He arose from his bearskin seat, clasped his arms around each one, laid his head upon one, then upon the other's shoulder, and shed tears copiously, expressing great gratitude for what we had done. It was some time before we were released; then his three wives gathered around and gave thanks as did also his noble looking son who had married the captive white girl heretofore spoken of. Saginaw offered us bear skins, ponies, crosses, Indian trinkets, moccasins made by his daughter, elegantly adorned with porcupine quills, bead bags and many Indian valuables, all of which were refused. More than fifty Indians, squaws and children gathered around to express their thanks. A few squaws a short distance away were preparing a feast. We were invited. The old chief marshalled them all in a circle, came for us, took the lead, and Indian file marched up to the circle which opened and let us into the centre, followed by his wives and

60

son, where we were seated on benches and partook heartily of soup, served in the skulls of bears and eat with wooden spoons. What the soup was made of we knew not but afterwards ascertained it was dog. It was well seasoned and excellent. This made us famous with all the Indians and their love and adoration was shown in various ways.

# CHAPTER XI.

*Saginaw Sick—Turning Doctor—Indian Mode of Curing Diseases-Narrow Escape of Gosa.*

Nothing of importance passed for a few days. We were on exceedingly good terms with the Indians. Meeting them in the forest they would greet us in the most friendly manner. We both felt at home in their wigwams and could vie with them in eating coon and muskrat soup out of bear or human skulls. Getting belated on one of our expeditions we found comfortable quarters with them. On one occasion Saginaw was quite ill and he sent a messenger on a pony, leading another, for us to call and see him. We were well supplied with various kinds of medicines which the Indians had heretofore refused to touch. Mounting the pony, we left the Captain, whose mission was to bring in a deer that day.

The distance was about two miles and we soon reached there and a dozen Indian boys were ready to greet us. One of his squaws received us with joy and took charge of the pony. The old chief lay on his bear skins in great pain and had a high fever. Fever powders were administered and he soon became quiet. We tarried over four hours, passing our time with their bows and arrows. Having practiced considerable, we surprised by them throwing our cap into the air and hitting it on its descent.

Leaving Saginaw in good condition with plenty

of medicines, with full directions, he soon recovered. This was our first patient and we were the great physician of the forest. After this we had our hands full. If any thing was the matter, we were needed and it became necessary to recommend their own remedies, which were first, dig a hole in the ground and place a kettle in it half full of water; cut up a lot of hemlock boughs for the water and then put in heated stone and create a steam, over which the patient is placed and covered with blankets, excepting the head, and thus they would steam them for an hour. When taken out they are wrapped in blankets and compelled to lay in the wigwam several hours before they stir, except to partake of tea made of bitter root. This generally answered their purpose. Still, we occasionally had to act as physician to keep peace.

Gosa was sick, and he was very sick, too. He had waded the river, set a trap and caught an otter for us, and he was the clever Indian. His niece brought us a pony and we hastened to see him. Yes, "poor old Gosa," as he was called, was in danger, having a high fever, breathing short, and stiffened all over, and was near lung fever. Fever powders were administered and he was wrapped in hot wet blankets, given hot hemlock tea, hot stone to his feet, and in two hours he was in a perspiration, and taking his bitter root he soon recovered. After this our fame spread far and wide among the Indians as the "great medicine man."

Not many days after this, we started out one morning after a deer. There had been a light snow over night and the bushes were loaded. Up the river, on the east side, was a thicket of small hemlock.

Here a deer could always be found and the tracks were plenty and fresh. Cautiously moving and peering in every direction, expecting every moment to get a shot, we saw a movement between the bent boughs, not larger than our hand. Quick as thought we took deadly aim, the cap burst, but the rifle failed to go off. Gosa lifted himself up; his porcupine cap, ornamented with feathers, was upon his head. It was an aim at him, who was our best forest friend. Had the rifle gone off he would have been shot through the body, and there was something strange about it for the next trial it did not fail. Gosa wept like a child when he learned how near we came to shooting him, and our feelings we cannot describe. He was a great favorite with all; had we killed him we never could have convinced the tribe it was by a mistake, and we would have been compelled to leave the forest. When it became known, many thought we could not be relied upon, that we were a dangerous white man, and there was more or less fear of us for a few days and until a meeting of Indians was called and Gosa explained the whole matter and told what friends we were and how much I had done for him. Saginaw, too, was at the meeting and he told a plain story how he once shot an Indian by a similar mistake, but he did not die. This was entirely satisfactory and confidence was fully restored.

# CHAPTER XII.

*A Deer Shot in His Bed—A Pursuit for a Buck—
Lost in a Swamp-The Value of a Match-A Perilous
Night.*

"Captain, there are fresh deer tracks between
here and the spring," said I early one morning as we
returned with a pail of water, "and I propose to get
one before breakfast," seizing our rifle. "Yes, but
I'll have breakfast in half an hour or so," said the
Captain. "I'll be here on time, and if you hear me
shoot come out and help me drag one in," said I,
jokingly. "Yes, yes," said the Captain laughing.

Out we went, and in less than thirty rods we saw
a fine doe lying down, and she was shot dead in her
bed. But a few steps off a fine buck jumped up, and
ere we could load was out of reach. By a cautious
pursuit we got in a shot at long range, but drew
blood freely and followed on, but knowing we would
be late to breakfast we retraced our steps for the doe,
and much to our surprise there was nothing left but
a small piece of skin which we took back for a cushion
to the shaving horse. The wolves had carried it all
off. This could not be believed until the Captain
examined the ground.

Breakfast being over we resolved to pursue the
wounded buck. Taking the track, the blood showed
he had a serious wound, and we had not gone far ere
he sprang up and dashed off, getting a second, but it

seems not a fatal shot. Thus we pursued this wounded buck far off from our lodge until the shadows of night began to set in, and we saw there was danger of not getting to our lodge. The day was cloudy and we had no idea how far we were from our camp. Our compass told us which way to steer our course to strike Rabbit river, and we hastened on as speedy as possible. But darker and darker it grew. Old Jim set up his great bass howl in the same place he always did, and we knew we must be a long distance off for he was between us and the lodge. If we could reach Rabbit river before dark we were safe for we knew of an Indian encampment up that river, but the distance to it seemed too great. Coming to a tamarack swamp we made up our mind our only salvation was to strike a fire, for the wolves were on our track and when darkness fairly set in an attack was certain. We gathered a lot of dry tamarack poles and kindlings but to our sorrow we could not find a match. Every pocket was searched in vain. We tried rubbing dry sticks together, but could not succeed in getting any thing but sparks. We determined to discharge our rifle and load with powder and tow, which we had in our game bag, which would set the tow on fire. After doing so and taking the tow out of the bag a solitary match dropped from it into the snow which we seized with the utmost care. Preparing well for a fire we lit the match, set the tow on fire and the dry bark and sticks were soon going, and as darkness fairly set in we had a fire which illuminated the wilderness for a long distance. We listened for the signal gun in vain, we were beyond hearing it. Every short time we would fire our own gun, but it was useless. The wolves surrounded us in large numbers, but the fire was our protector. Sometimes when it became a little dim they would approach nearer. Their howls and growls were terrific. They would often have a fight among themselves, and their clear voices would ring for miles around. When their eyes were turned towards us they would glisten by the light of the fire, and occasionally we would shoot as near as possible between them. The noise of a rifle would still them but for a moment when a louder and more terrific howling would be set up. Thus all the long night we worked to keep up the fire, and dry tamarack near us was getting scarce. To venture out too far was certain food for them. On one occasion, one wolf more daring than the rest, while we were procuring a dead tree four or five rods from the fire, came so near we heard him snuff. Turning around we saw his glaring eyes not over three rods off. Dropping our pole we took good aim at his eyes and he fell dead, but we did not know it then. He was apparently crouched for a spring when we shot. We only knew the eyes disappeared. It was a cold and dreary night. We had fixed a place to sit down, and in a minute we fell asleep and fell off. This awakened us and we dare not sit down again. A few frozen roasted potatoes were found in our pocket, which we thawed out and eat, which were refreshing. Daylight dawned at last, and as it grew lighter the pack drew off and their noise was hushed. We went to see the effect of our shots and found the venturesome wolf dead in the snow. Those farther off had been hit, as seen by blood, but not fatally. All around and within eight rods and less the snow was completely tread down, and here and there blood and hair, caused either by their fights or bullets, by bullets we imagined, for we sent not less than ten in their direction.

It was a night of terror, long and dreary. Almost ready to surrender to fatigue we pursued our northern course slowly and sadly, for even then we began to think we must perish alone in the forest. At last we struck the river and took new courage. Here there was a half beaten Indian trail and our steps were quickened. Onward we pressed and at last we beheld one of the most beautiful pictures the eye could imagine. It was smoke curling up among the trees. It was an Indian encampment and we were greeted with a hearty welcome. Here were those whom we had chastised for robbery. We told them our story, and two young bucks started for the wolf with ponies, and in less than an hour he was brought in.

They feasted us on their best—boiled muskrat, corn bread and potatoes. They brought up their best ponies and one strapped the wolf on, took the lead, and in an hour we reached our lodge. It was about 10 a.m. and the Captain had taken our track, but a shot from our rifle was answered near a mile off and he speedily returned and it was a joyful meeting for he never expected to see us alive. We remained in camp three days before we recovered sufficiently to be out.

# CHAPTER XIII.

*An Expedition after Beaver—Bed on Hemlock Boughs—A Chase and Capture of a Wolf—An Indian Killed.*

It was in March. The snow had entirely disappeared in many places. We had just completed our breakfast when Su-na-gun suddenly entered in quite an excited state. "What now, Su-na-gun?" asked the Captain. "Nene kin-a-poo ma-quaw!" (I've killed a bear.) He wanted us to go and help drag him in. We had heard a gun not far off, but it was nothing uncommon. Quickly we were prepared. Not half a mile distant lay bruin, but already the wolves had found him, but they had not devoured him, although he was considerably torn to pieces. We soon took off his hide and hung him up in quarters on trees, and the Indian took him as he desired. This over, Su-na-gun said, "Me know where there be beaver, but me dare not tell white man, Indian kill me." He could not be pursuaded to tell us where the beaver dam was only it was on a stream down the river that ran in from the east. It was resolved to start on a tramp for it the next day and four traps were procured, a sheet for a tent, two days rations were prepared, consisting of venison and roasted potatoes. Bright and early we were off in the morning for the river, followed down on the east side, struck a stream and followed it up a long distance, sought another and followed it down. When we struck the river the first day was spent. We sought a large fallen tree for a head-board and here we gathered hemlock boughs, which were plenty on the banks, and made a bed, built a fire with dry logs at our feet, propped up the center of the sheet, fastened down the edges, eat our cold supper and crawled under the sheet. Hemlock boughs make a splendid bed and one upon which it is believed no person can take cold. No one ever slept sounder than we did until about 2 o'clock in the morning, when Rhodes gave us a nudge and said in a whisper, "listen!" The snuffing of wolves was close to the log at our heads. Our fire had nearly died out and they ventured up on the dark side. We sprang out speedily. The Captain seized a fire-brand and threw it at them and at the same time I let go my rifle. This put them to flight in all directions. In a few minutes they seemed to have all congregated and such a howling was very rare. Replenishing our fire we slept soundly the balance of the night.

At daylight we pursued our journey, following up and down streams, but abandoned pursuit the second day in time to reach our lodge. Although we had traveled a long distance, we were not more than three miles from camp. Taking a direct route we soon came to the swamp where we had traps and found one of them gone. The chain was so short the wolf had gnawed off the end of the spring pole and escaped with only the trap and chain. We hung up our baggage on trees and began to circle the swamp. The Captain soon started him, and cried out, "here he is!" At the same time came the report of his rifle and a cry, "cut across, he has turned up the river!"

I did so, and when I struck the river and cast an eye up towards a bend, the wolf was plainly visible; the descending sun shining upon him, he glistened like silver. He was carrying the heavy trap by the left fore leg, evidently much fatigued. By a short cut the Captain headed us off and gave another shot as he crossed the river on a sleeper, the last remnant of a bridge built by government surveyors. I kept up a regular Indian trot, crossed the river in the same place and kept a constant gain on him. The heavy trap was too much for him. His tongue hung out and he surrendered and wheeled towards us. I paused and so did he. When I approached toward him he did the same toward us. Being not more than three rods apart, we took a sure aim at his throat and he fell, but he lay, with his head up. The Captain came up, took a rest, fired at his head, the ball passing over the top of his ears. I had approached within a few feet of him when the Captain says, "keep back and load up for he will come for you when he gets rest." Before I got a ball down he stretched out his neck and the blood burst out a stream, the artery being severed the first shot. In a few minutes his hide was off and he measured six feet six inches from the end of his nose to the end of his tail. He was a monster, but very poor for he was lame, having been in our trap before and lost the ball of his foot and nails. It was now about dark; the wolves began their music and having no torches we hurried to our lodge and when we reached there a pack of wolves were not far behind. We will here add that the next morning we visited the carcass of the wolf to see if wolves had eaten it, but found they had not. It was completely covered with honey bees pouring in and out of a beech tree near by. This confirmed what we had heard, that wolves would not devour each other unless upon the point of starvation.

We were satisfied this was old Jim for his howlings were heard no more.

Relative to the beaver dam, the Indians went there, caught two beaver, got into a quarrel and one Indian was killed.

# CHAPTER XIV.

*A Bear Killed—A Midnight Alarm—Narrow Escape
from a Shot in the Dark.*

It was in March; our venison was getting low;
the Captain left us to go to the upper traps and he
was not expected home that night. About thirty rods
from the lodge poles had been placed in the crotches
of trees, forming a scaffold about twenty feet high
over a deer runway. Thither we went just before
sunset and took our station on the poles, keeping a
watch both ways. We had not been there long before
a monster black bear made his appearance. It was
the first we had seen. He moved along on the trail
slowly, looking first one way, then another. It is
evident he smelt our tracks for when he came under
us he stopped and in a moment a bullet broke through
his skull. He whirled around several times while we
were reloading. It was evident he had his death
wound, but another shot cut his throat and he died
in ten minutes. Here was another dilemma. He
would weigh near three hundred pounds and to
leave him there would be food for the wolves in an
hour. A large fire was built, we went to the lodge,
procured torches and went for Mr. Chambers. He
readily hastened to our assistance and we dragged
him into the lodge amid the terrific tumult of wolves
and owls. Mr. Chambers returned and we retired for
the night.

It was midnight when we were aroused by the most unearthly yells ever yet heard in the forest. It seemed as if a hundred Indians were screaming and very near our lodge. We seized our rifle, mounted. on the top of our cabin and fired into the midst of the tumult, as we had done before to a pack of wolves. "Hold on there!" exclaimed the familiar voice of brother Daniel; "we're coming to make you a call." "All right, come in. Are either of you wounded?" "No, but a close call. We knew you were alone and we took it into our heads to give you a scare and came three miles with torches to do it." "Such a move at midnight would have done it once, but you know all fear of any thing vanishes after one has been with wolves and Indians as long as you fellows have. We are all a pretty close shot by sound and it is best not to get up any night scares." The bullet had grazed the top of Daniel's ear and it was the last time such an attempt was made.

# CHAPTER XV.

*A Trip for Porcupine—Twenty Killed—A Visit from
a Bear—Potatoes Scarce.*

Porcupines were so numerous and so useless
to us that we seldom killed one. Go in any direction
and there they were. The good old Indian Gosa
wanted a lot of them, and he had been so kind to us
we volunteered to kill them. He called by appoint-
ment at an early hour in the morning with his pony
and a sack made of deer skin large enough to hold
forty or more. There was no trouble in finding them
for they were quite plenty, and we were not over four
hours killing twenty or more.

On our return to camp we came upon a party of
Indians who were cutting a bee tree. It was a dead
pine tree about a foot through. It was a mere shell.
The bees went in about fifteen feet high. In cutting
they found old candied honey at the butt. It was full
of solid honey over thirty feet high and did not contain less than five hundred pounds. They were
several days in carrying it off. They presented us
with three muhkuks full, which became very ac-
ceptable on pancakes. This honey had to be strongly
barricaded with heavy trees to keep the wolves off
for they were fond of everything sweet. It was with
maple sugar Gosa caught a wolf for us that hung
around his wigwam.

On our return from camp we found our door

open and tread cautiously to catch a thief. On looking in, a large black bear had found the potatoes in the hole under our bed and was devouring them as speedily as possible. We closed the door upon him, and had him fast. This done we climbed upon the top and had a fine view of the black monster. He made a desperate leap against the door and then at us, and as he did that his hind feet got into live coals which made him desperate, and he raved and tore around the lodge. It was our desire to rope him and secure him alive, but we found it an impossibility, and he was finally dispatched by the Captain with two shots in the head. Indian Gosa and Su-na-gun skinned him and took the carcass excepting one quarter which we desired for our worthy neighbor Chamber's use.

Every thing in our lodge was now in great confusion. Our bed, our cooking utensils, were scattered all over the lodge. Our plates, were overturned and had to be washed up. An hour or more was spent in cleaning after bruin before we could get a meal.

In the mean time we had a call from Mr. Chambers, who brought us potatoes, having heard by an Indian of our loss. But notwithstanding the bear had devoured many, still we had plenty and he enjoyed a venison supper with us.

# CHAPTER XVI.

*A Visit from Noonday—Happy Meeting—Prayers—
Music, etc.*

Noonday and Saginaw were great friends. They
had been together in various bloody battles, in
massacres, and raids. History has never recorded
and never will the horrible scenes of cruelty to
captive men, women and children, for none but
Indians knew and they were silent on the subject.
Some historians endeavor to prove Tecumseh was
opposed to the tortures and massacres of prisoners,
but he was deceptive, being the fiercest in the
slaughter and scalping of those in his power, without regard to age or sex. This meeting was arranged
by Adaniram and we were anxious to witness it and
the two hunter boys were invited to be present and at
the feast. Noonday was a convert to the Christian
religion under the teachings of missionary Slater
and he was very anxious for the conversion of
Saginaw. The 5th of March, 1840, Noonday mounted
his decorated pony for the journey, and he arrived
at his wigwam, a distance from near Gull prairie of
about twenty miles. Young and old had assembled
to receive the warrior chieftain, and when he have in
sight the yell of joy and welcome resounded through
the forest.

The tent of Saginaw was elegantly ornamented
with various Indian trinkets. The pipe of Tecumseh

was most conspicuous. As he dismounted, a son of Saginaw's took him by the arm and conducted him to the wigwam where he was received with open arms. They continued in each others embrace for five minutes. Then his three wives with his son advanced and there was a happy greeting.

Noonday knew the writer of this sketch, he having attended the meetings of the Slater mission, near the borders of Gull prairie, and near the county line between Kalamazoo and Barry county, Mich., several Sundays and listened to his prayers, and he extended both hands to us. He was then introduced to Captain Rhodes as one of the brave boys, at whom he gazed with his dark and piercing eye, in silence, for some time, a gaze which would have made one with less courage, falter. This over, there was a general greeting. The chief would take the little ones, toss them high in the air and catch them as they came down. Finally they sit down upon the carpet of furs and talked over the times long ago, without any apparent reserve for our presence, and in some respects corroborated portions of the written history of the

### MASSACRE AT THE RIVER RAISIN.

Tecumseh, Noonday, Saginaw, Sunagun, Gosa, and their party of braves were starting on a raid when news came that a company had left Detroit to meet troops on their way from Ohio, at Frenchtown, on the River Raisin, and they rushed to join the British and Indians who were in possession of that town. Tecumseh and Noonday flew to the Wabash where they were to be joined by two hundred and hurry to Frenchtown, but they did not reach there until the conflict was over. Chief Roundhead and

Spitlog were in command of the Indians there. A fierce and bloody battle was fought. The British, under General Procter, were victorious and the Indians had many scalps. A portion of the Americans, still behind pickets, held out. Procter assured them if they would surrender they should be protected, otherwise he would turn them over for the Indians to burn and scalp. This alarmed General Winchester who sent word for a surrender, which

MASSACRE AT RIVER RAISIN.

they did under the promise they should be protected. The terms of surrender maddened the Indians for they were suffering for a slaughter. The British troops started for Malden, accompanied by the Indians, but so enraged did Saginaw and other chiefs become, they turned back, set fire to the town and dragged the sick and wounded from their beds, scalped them and threw them into the flames. Here Saginaw was scalping a man when a woman rushed

79

in to beg for his life; she was instantly killed and scalped. Here he exhibited the scalp of the woman heretofore described. Saginaw was one of the principal leaders in this massacre. His voice could be heard, "on to the slaughter!" At fort Meigs he also got many scalps.

Capt. Rhodes sat listening to the tales of the two chiefs with clenched teeth. The feast was prepared and all partook heartily. Noonday made a speech and said: "There is war talked of now between the Americans and the British. Now the Indians would draw like a yoke of oxen together with the Americans. They be our friends. Me no more go to war. My people they all gone. The white man he tell us of the happy hunting ground in the distance. Saginaw he be with me in this world and now he go join the good Indian and go with me to the happy hunting grounds."

Saginaw appeared considerably affected. "He was delighted to see his old friend, Noonday. Some good che-mo-ke-men (white men) and some very bad. They drive us from the graves of our fathers. They load them in wagons and force our mothers, sons and daughters from their dear old homes towards the setting sun, beyond the father of waters which we know nothing of. They rob us of our hunting grounds and destroy our forest homes. The British no do that. Happy Indians in Canada. Go-da-see came and see me and he say good hunting ground and good white man in Canada. The white men here (pointing to us) they be good, they do much for Indian." He then rehearsed to Noonday what had been done and sat down.

Capt. Rhodes said, "he was glad to be present here. He liked the good Indian; liked to hear the words of Noonday, how he would help the Americans in another war. Saginaw he go to Canada, he help the British—("No, no!" said Saginaw—) he then be a bad Indian, but he say no, then he be good Indian and he liked Saginaw and all the good Indians. He would be always good to them and he was glad to meet them."

Noonday spent the night with Saginaw as did also the two hunters. The evening was spent in singing songs, dancing and story telling. Before retiring Noonday offered up a fervent prayer for Saginaw, his family and his tribe.

# CHAPTER XVII.

*The War and Scalp Dance in full Indian Costume.*

Saginaw's wigwam was large. The fire was in the centre on the ground. All slept in a circle on furs, covered with blankets, with feet towards the fire, and it was very comfortable. Sometimes the wolves would prowl very near, but the Indians had no fear of them. They called them their fellow hunters, yet they were very careful not be be far out in the woods after dark.

At early dawn the squaws had prepared venison and fish and all partook with a relish, but Noonday did not forget his morning devotions and his blessings before eating. Mr. Slater had instructed him in this, and he was a most devoted Christian.

It was our earnest desire to see the war and scalp dance. Noonday at first objected, saying it awakened hostile feelings, but he finally consented as Saginaw desired to please us. In an hour twenty Indians were in costume, with bows and arrows attached to them, and hatchets in their hands. They were painted and ornamented in fine style. Noonday gave the order and a circle was formed in a moment. In the centre was a young squaw beating on an Indian drum,

SCALP DANCE.

keeping exact time. Each one took the same steps and flourished the tomahawk in the same manner. The Indian war whoop was most thrilling, and even awakened in Noonday fierce passions. No one can witness such a dance without a shudder.

But if this was terrific the scalp dance was more so. They at once formed in a similar manner, with two squaw drummers, and prepared for the dance. Most of them had a scalp on the end of a pole, and they would flourish them at the same moment and sing most blood curdling songs. In the midst of the tumult, old Saginaw seized a pole upon the end of which was the scalp of the long black haired woman. He broke through the line and was received with fearful yells and flourished his scalp far above all others. The old chief understood it to perfection. At his word all would pause for a moment and by a move of his arm all would start. In a moment the poles bearing the scalps would change hands, those having none receiving them with a yell signifying, "I have taken none but will!" It had been many years since Noonday had witnessed the dance and he seemed to enjoy it exceedingly, occasionally slapping his hands and joining in the song. Yet, after all, he would break down in sorrow at the past and it scarcely seemed possible that such a savage, so cruel, so fond of torture, could be tamed down to such meekness and humility by the teachings of a missionary. But such is the power of the Christian religion.

This over we retired to the wigwam and all were seated. Noonday was handed the Tecumseh pipe. He at once recognized it and turned it over to view it in every part.

The writer then asked Noonday what he did with Tecumseh's tomahawk which he told him a year ago went into his hands after he fell? "Nene son took 'em beyond the waters to the setting sun."

Saginaw was asked what became of the war cap which he had. He said as before that it was torn to pieces in a strife for it."

# CHAPTER XVIII.

*Col. Johnson Killed Tecumseh-Noonday saw him at Washington.*

In June, 1885, the author furnished the following which was published in the Century Magazine:

SIR: I notice in the January number of your very interesting magazine an article by Bonjamin C. Griswold relative to the killing of Tecumseh by Richard M. Johnson  It reminds me of an interview which I had with Noonday, Chief of the Ottowa tribe, about the year 1838.  The chief was six feet high, broad-shouldered, well proportioned, with broad, high cheek-bones, piercing black eyes, and coarse black hair which hung down upon his shoulders, and he possessed wonderful muscular power.  He was converted to the Christian religion by a Baptist missionary named Slater, who was stationed about three miles north of Gull Prairie, in the county of Kalamazoo, Michigan.  Just over the county line and in the edge of Barry county, this chief and about one hundred and fifty of his tribe were located and instructed in farming.  A church was erected which answered for a school-house, and here, residing near them, I attended their church and listened to the teachings of Mr. Slater in the Indian dialect, and to the earnest prayers of this brave old chief.  To get a history of any Indian who fought on the side of the British has ever been a difficult task; but through the Rev. Mr. Slater I succeeded to a limited extent, in getting a sketch from this old chief of the battle of the Thames, in which he was engaged. I copy from a diary:

"After rehearsing the speech which Tecumseh made to his warriors previous to the engagement and how they all felt, that they fought to defend Tecumseh more than for the British, he was asked:

" 'Were you near Tecumseh when he fell?'

" 'Yes; directly on his right.'

" 'Who killed him?'

" 'Richard M. Johnson.'

" 'Give us the circumstances.'

" 'He was on a horse, and the horse fell over a log, and Tecumseh, with uplifted tomahawk, was about to dispatch him, when he drew a pistol from his holster and shot him in the breast, and he fell dead on his face. I seized him at once and with the assistance of Saginaw, bore him from the field. When he fell the Indians stopped fighting and the battle ended. We laid him down on a blanket in a wigwam, and we all wept, we loved him so much. I took his hat and tomahawk.

" 'Where are they now?'

" 'I have his tomahawk and Saginaw his hat.'

" 'Could I get them?'

" 'No; Indian keep them.'

" 'How did you know it was Johnson who killed him?'

" 'General Cass took me to see the Great Father, Van Buren, at Washington. I went to the great wigwam, and when I went in I saw the same man I see in battle, the same man I see kill Tecumseh. I had never seen him since, but I knew it was him. I look him in the face and said, "Kene kin-a-poo Tecumseh," that is, "You killed Tecumseh." Johnson replied that he never knew who it was, but a powerful Indian approached him and he shot him with his pistol. "That was Tecumseh. I see you do it." ' "

Noonday finished his story of Tecumseh by telling of his noble traits, the tears meanwhile trickling down his cheeks. There is no doubt of the truth of his unvarnished tale.

D.B. COOK

Editor of "The Niles Mirror."

Niles, Mich., Dec. 24, 1884.

The speech of Tecumseh, as remembered by Noonday, above referred to, was delivered in a standing position on a log. He said: "Warriors, we are all armed for the conflict. The Americans are our enemies and they seek to deprive us of our loved homes. They seek to destroy us. The British are our friends. They will give us our homes and make us happy. This land belongs to the red warriors and the Americans would rob us of this and send us beyond the Wabash. Let us defend our homes and the scalps we gather in this day we will offer up to the Great Spirit. Follow me and victory is ours."

———

A STORY BY SAGINAW—*How he got Wounded—A Curious Circumstance.*

The Indians would climb trees in Canada the better to secrete themselves and watch out for

American scouts, and when within range, shoot them. On one occasion he saw a soldier near the shore of lake Erie, skulking along, peering in every direction. He gave him a shot and he dodged behind a big rock, he having missed him. Being mostly hid by the body of the tree, the scout had no chance for a shot at him, even when he was reloading his gun, but he stuck his hat up a little above the rock and Saginaw put a bullet through it and it fell. Being sure he had killed him, he hastened down from the tree and rushed for his scalp. When near the rock the soldier darted out and gave him a shot at close range. The ball grazed the top of the hip bone, taking a small piece off and cutting the flesh. It crippled him considerable but he succeeded in making his escape. A second shot was given before he got out of range which grazed his neck, taking off a piece of the skin.

It is a curious circumstance that many years afterwards the writer should know who this soldier was.

Uncle Samuel Hall was a native of Milton, Litchfield county, Connecticut. He volunteered early in the war of 1812, and his regiment was ordered to Buffalo. It was a long and dreary march from Albany. His brother, Daniel Hall, and friends never heard from him for near thirty years and supposed he was killed. At last he was found by his nephew, Salmon C. Hall, and by him brought to Gull prairie in Kalamazoo county, where he resided for several years with him and finally with Reuben Spencer, a son-in-law of Salmon C., where he died about 1864. He had spent most of his time since the war in Canada, as a gardener. The writer formed his acquaintance at Gull prairie. He was full of interesting war stories and among others he told how he fooled an Indian. He said an Indian shot at him from a tree. The ball passed between his arm and body and struck on a flat rock in the edge of the water, leaving a streak of lead on the rock which he saw many years after the war was over. He dodged behind a big rock directly in his front, put his hat on the point of his bayonet and stuck it a little above the top of the rock and the Indian put a bullet through it and it fell. "I saw him coming," said Uncle Sam, "with a whoop and a yell, with his scalping knife and hatchet. When within two rods I dodged out and gave him a shot and he wheeled and hobbled off. I could have bayoneted him, but supposed other Indians near and under the cover of the rock reloaded and had another shot. I know I hit him for he put his hand to his neck and passed out of sight. I was satisfied there was one Indian less."

"No, Uncle Sam," said I, "that Indian is alive now." I then rehearsed the story of Saginaw, and he resolved to see him.

# CHAPTER XIX.

## VARIOUS INDIAN STORIES.

STORY BY NOONDAY—*Raids into Ohio.*

Tecumseh was a great and powerful Indian, bigger than Saginaw. Alone he would go among the different tribes and get them to join him. He went into Ohio, Kentucky and far south, and learned the whole country. Thus becoming familiar, he selected ten braves and made a dash into Ohio and back in a few days with women and children they would capture in fields or wherever they could with safety. Children, too young to manage well, had their brains dashed out against trees. The women were compelled to astride ponies behind Indians and flee with them or be pierced with arrows. The captives were hurried to Malden, in Canada. Here, on different raids, they gathered twenty and then hurried them through Canada down to Niagara falls. On the trip, they were tortured in various ways. At the falls, some were torn open, scalped and thrown over the precipice; others were only scalped before they were thrown over. A British officer, on one occasion, interfered and stopped the scalping and torture but permitted them to be thrown into the waters. This made them indignant and they resolved to abandon them, but the matter was settled with tobacco and fire water.

On one of these raids they were pursued by a

band of whites. They were on their return with five prisoners, and when near the end of their journey they encamped in woods, were resting themselves and their ponies, partaking of refreshments, little dreaming of pursuit, when suddenly a large squad of white men dashed in upon them about midnight, and by the light of their camp fires, killed four out of ten, and wounded two, and retook the prisoners, consisting of one young man, two women and two girls. We escaped with our wounded to our ponies a short distance off. In the darkness they dare not pursue. We crept cautiously around, but the fires were put out and they had left. We could not carry away our dead. One of the wounded died the next day; the other recovered and here he is. Here he showed the scar where was wounded by a ball in the calf of his right leg.

"How did you get these prisoners?"

"Always on our return. One go to a house to get something to eat; the others hid away. He get all he want; he be friendly; he see who all there; he make a sign, and we all come down upon them and we get them and provisions—all the family but one and he gone to the war.

———

STORY BY GOSA—*Capture of Three American Scouts—Escape of One—Revenge.*

Ten of us were on a rampage one day and sneaked around and captured three American scouts. One of them was a very tall man, taller than Indian had ever seen, and we made him run the gauntlet to see

91

him fall. A long string of us formed large circles, three feet apart, would stand and he must run between us at the top of his speed. When he got under headway we would trip him up to see him fall, but he must keep going or be pricked with arrows. This was our daily fun for some time.

"We finally got him on a pair of skates on the river and he could not stand. He would get up and fall in all ways and we enjoyed the fun exceedingly. He kept working off from us little by little and finally he got up and swifter than the eagle he sped away from us. Arrows and bullets followed him but he escaped. He was a swift skater and had fooled us by his falls."

"The other two did not fare so well." Here Gosa paused. "Well Gosa, 'tis all over now; we are friends and we like to hear your stories." "Me no like to tell all," said Gosa. "O, yes, all good Indians now. Chemo-ke-men (white men) like Indian now," said we. "We held a council after tall man escaped. Sag-wa be very mad; he tell how white man deceive 'em; he said burn one and cut the other to pieces. Saginaw he say take off skin and burn 'em. Su-na-gun he go with Sag-wa. Noonday he go with Sag-wa and all the Indians they go with him, and so we tied the smallest man's hands to a tree up over his head, lifted him up so his feet did not hit the ground, put sharp pitch pine sticks in his flesh, set them on fire and danced around him. He made a great fuss, but the more he writhed and cried the more the Indian yelled and danced."

"But where was Tecumseh all this time?"

"He, with two others, had left us to join General Brock." "What became of the other prisoner?"

"The other one, during the night, made believe he was asleep, broke his bands around his feet, leaped up, seized Indian gun, killed Sag-wa with the bayonet, and ran to make his escape; Indian shot and broke his leg and he no run. We bound him to a log and each Indian he cut out a small piece of him. They cut off his nose first, then his ears, took out one eye, then the other. He very bad white man; he kill Sag-wa. Each one to cut so he not bleed too fast for they gloried in his torture. They corded his toes and cut them off. The same with his legs and arms until they reached his body. Finally Su-na-gun he said how he kill Sag-wa and cut his throat. Saginaw he got his scalp.

## SKETCHES.

Saginaw delighted to talk about the capture of the little girl at Buffalo; how he protected her; dressed her in fawn skins, ornamented her with beads and feathers in the most gaudy Indian costumes. She soon became accustomed to their ways, could shoot an arrow, row a canoe and catch fish equal to any of them. Occasionally she would speak of her mother and old home when she was upbraided.

———

Tecumseh, Saginaw, Su-na-gun, Gosa and ten others were in Canada, far away, as they supposed, from American scouts. They had been encamped there a few days to rest and refresh themselves on the banks of a lake. "They had venison in abundance and were in the midst of a feast when a large squad of soldiers rushed from the bushes upon us, killed four of our number, wounded several others, captured our guns, ammunition, and all we had, including several ponies. We scattered in all directions. Excepting our hatchets, we were entirely unarmed."

"I, with Tecumseh," said Saginaw, "broke quickly by them. Tecumseh fell over a log and severely injured his right shoulder, making it useless for several days."

The British supplied us with new arms.

------

### GOSA'S BEAR STORY.

One time he pitched his wigwam, with others of his tribe, at the outlet of Thornapple lake, in Barry county. It was in 1837, when there was but one log house in Hastings, and that a hotel, where the author remained over night with his companion named Whitcomb. There was splendid hunting in this vicinity. On one of Gosa's excursions, a half wolf dog which he owned, was taught to follow cautiously in his footsteps, never being allowed to leave his place until some game was badly wounded; then wait a few minutes for game to bleed, he was placed upon the track and away he sped. The dog was very fleet and would soon overtake a deer that is weak from the loss of blood, and would either kill or worry them until he came up.

On one of his hunting trips his dog made a sudden leap from him and rushed with the utmost speed out of sight. It was not long before he discovered the cause, which was the fresh track of a large black bear. His bark was soon heard in the distance and hastening to him, bruin was found resting quietly in the crotch of a tree, watching the movements of the dog. Gosa did not take his usual precaution to climb a small tree, but stood on the ground, gave him a shot which brought him down. He rushed to him with his hunting knife to cut his throat and was immediately knocked down by the bear's fore-arm; before he could recover himself the bear was upon him, and fastening his teeth in his left arm, surrounded his body, and, lifting his hind feet up, tore his buckskin breeches and lacerted his limbs in a most fearful manner. While he was doing this, Gosa was using his knife with deadly effect, piercing the heart, which caused a speedy death on his person, and he was completely drenched in the bear's blood.

"But where was the dog all this time?"

While the struggle was going on the bear paid no attention to the dog that was snapping and biting him on all sides. Gosa, who was bleeding from his wounds, found it quite difficult to turn the bear off and stand upon his feet; he did so, however, and, leaving his rifle, started for his wigwam, giving, with all his strength, the Indian cry of distress. It was about one mile distant and he had not proceeded more than half way before he was compelled to rest from the loss of blood. Luckily an Indian who was hunting, heard his cry and hastening to him found he was in an exhausted condition. Leaving there and going for help, sending forth the cry of distress, he was soon met by six Indians who carried him speedily in and made a strong decoction of hemlock bark to bathe his wounds and stop the bleeding. His limbs were bound with such bandages as they had and it was three months before he enjoyed another hunt. He exhibited his scars and pointed to the skull of the bear.

## BY SAGINAW.

When the moon was full and the leaves had
fallen, I went with Tecumseh, Noonday, Sag-wa,
Gosa and a number of others, on ponies among the
Indians of Ohio and Kentucky. We held large meetings and many Indians agreed to appear at Malden
and join the British. But few of them did as they
agreed for General Harrison sent Indians on our
trail who told them we be their enemies and we
wanted them killed. When the moon was old we left
for Malden. It was our aim to capture all the prisoners we could and take them to Malden alive or
their scalps, for either of which we got a reward. We
were on the war path on our return. Sometimes we
found women and children husking corn in the
fields; on seeing us approach they would flee to
their log huts and barricade the doors and windows,
and so strong were they made it was difficult to
batter them down with hatchets. Chimneys were
made with sticks on the outside. On one occasion
where a family fled to the house a Delaware Indian,
who had joined us, climbed up on the outside to go
down the chimney. When part way down, a quantity
of sulphur was thrown upon the fire and he was
smothered and fell down upon the fire where he was
dispatched with an axe. We then tore the chimney
down to the ground, set fire to the house and captured
all the inmates, two women, two girls, a boy and a
baby. The little one was killed and left to the flames.
We lashed our captives to our ponies and galloped
off. When passing through a thicket we were fired
upon by a number of men in ambush. Three of our
ponies were killed and three of our company. I was
wounded here (showing his arm.) We lost all our

captives but a girl, but we were pursued so furiously by a few Kentuckians, who were mounted, that we took her scalp and dropped her. We then scattered, going in various directions, rendering pursuit impossible. It was some days before we all met at Malden. Gosa was wounded in his left arm. A ball passed through the cap of Tecumseh, grazing the top of his head and he laughed about it. It was evident we had been watched and they had prepared for our return and we fared badly.

Tecumseh was the last to come in and we all feared he was killed, but he went to the Wabash and brought in ten new recruits and two prisoners. When he made his appearance there was great rejoicing and General Brock ordered a salute.

---

BY SAGINAW—*Hull's Surrender.*

If we captured Detroit we were to have many scalps and much burning and plunder. Tecumseh he cross over with his warriors, Gen. Brock he follow and then we march toward the town. We expected big fight and were greatly surprised at the surrender of Gen. Hull at the first fire. When the man came out with the white flag, Indian yell big. We all thought Tecumseh knew beforehand about the surrender for he ordered the prisoners should be protected and he see the order enforced.

"Where was Tecumseh at the battle of Tippecanoe?" It was intended there should be no battle there until after his return with his warriors, Pawnees and others from the south. He had gathered over one hundred and fifty braves and was on his return when the battle was fought. Tecumseh was big with rage. He charged the prophet was the cause of the battle and he said "kill him!" and many said "kill him!" Tecumseh he be very mad; he stamp his feet; his braves, they pull out his hair and wanted his scalp, but Tecumseh he hear him cry for mercy, how he was deceived and say "let him go to his own wigwam, he be bad Indian."

# CHAPTER XX.

*Final Departure—A Farewell Feast.*

On the 20th of April, 1840 Capt. Rhodes and the writer called on Saginaw and informed him we should leave the forest April 28, and we requested him and his family to be present on the 26th at a feast; that he also invite twenty others of his choice, including Gosa and Noonday to be present. He expressed great sorrow at this announcement, but said he would be with us and bring others on that day. Mr. and Mrs. Chambers were also invited. Two deer were prepared for the occasion. Mrs. Chambers loaned us a large kettle, all her dishes, baked our bread, while Mr. Chambers furnished and pounded our corn, both doing all in their power to assist us. The time came and so did the company on ponies, dressed in the most gorgeous Indian costumes they possessed. Several squaws brought in muhkuks bear skulls, wooden spoons and forks. Noonday was ill and could not leave the Slater mission to go so far. Every thing was ready, consisting of roasted venison, corned bear, venison soup with boiled corn and potatoes. At one o'clock all sat down on poles, supported by shingle blocks, and covered with deer and wolf skins, the chief at the head on bear skins. The table was of boards furnished by Mr. Chambers.

There was fun at this table. Some would eat as much as possible and stop and sing an Indian song and at times all jump up, swing their arms and join in the chorus. They had been told to enjoy themselves in their own way. Adaniram, who had lived with white men, was full of jokes and fun which Saginaw and his wives did not seem to enjoy, but his son did exceedingly.

This over, Adaniram made a few brief remarks in the Indian tongue, telling them of the great benefits an English education had been to him, advising them to send their children to English schools; he closed by many thanks to the hunter boys whom he claimed had done them good.

Saginaw said: "He no like white man on Indian hunting ground, at first. They had been driven every where. He had no home no more for him or his. He thought bad of us when we came with our rifles for to stay; but he was much glad now we did stay. They did him good. They can sleep in his wigwam all the time. They go and we no more see 'em." The old chief embraced both. His wives, Adaniram, Gosa and all shook our hands, bid us good-by, mounted their ponies and left near sunset, making the wilderness ring with song as they went.

At the appointed time, Mr. Chambers conveyed us to Gull prairie, and thus ended our forest life. Nine wolves, two bear, (number of deer not kept,) and various kinds of other animals were captured. More precious than all was the restoration to health.

# APPENDIX.

*A Visit to the Old Hunting Grounds—Interview with Henry Gilbert, the Founder of the Kalamazoo Gazette—A Thriving Village-Sketch of the Family of the First Settler, Nelson Chambers—The Splendid Artesian Wells—The Present Business Men, etc.*

Near half a century had passed since companion Rhodes and the writer left the forest, and before closing this little historical work it seemed necessary to visit the grounds where the scenes took place, and as its first chapter announced our reception by Nelson Chambers, the first and only white settler in that part of the county of Allegan, the author felt anxious to know whether Mr. and Mrs. C. were still there and their destiny and that of his family.

March 14, 1889, found us on the Central road bound for Kalamazoo. On landing there our first business was to seek out the first editor and founder of the Kalamazoo Gazette, Henry Gilbert, who gave us our first position in western Michigan on a newspaper in 1837. We were not long in reaching his beautiful dwelling and the door bell called a matronly appearing lady, who informed us Mr. G. would be in soon and invited us to a seat where we pleasantly spent a few minutes, when Mr. Gilbert appeared. Grasping him by the hand,—"Do you recognize me?" Gazing with earnestness, he could not. He was reminded of many transactions in by-gone days, of his old office and bookstore, of the departure of two young men for the wilderness, and he well remembered all. Perhaps we did not have a jovial time in rehearsing the scenes of the past. In the meantime his estimable wife prepared a sump-tuous dinner. Mr. Gilbert, although near 80, is full of life and vigor and highly esteemed, as he ever was, for his integrity and honor. We have never seen a neater or more delightful dwelling than his, pat-terned after one he saw in California.

Taking our departure, we boarded a car on the G. R. and I. Railroad, we proceeded twenty-eight miles, to what is now known as the village of Wayland, in the township of Wayland, Allegan county, where we arrived at 3:09 p.m. The first to encounter is huge piles of lumber, turned out from a saw mill nearby, and, of course, the omnibus men, seeking to rake in the dimes. A ride of half a mile brought us to the Wayland Hotel, erected many years ago by Nelson Chambers, the first settler, who, while the plank road was in existence, made a handsome fortune keeping travelers who would invariably stop with him on their way to Grand Rapids. The railroad materially interfered with his business. This hotel is now kept by his son, George Bennett Chambers, and better and more wholesome fare cannot be had at any hotel in a country town. Mr. C. was at his farm of 320 acres, about three miles out. (The beaver we sought were on this farm.)

Could it be possible this was the same ground where once the wild savages roamed, the wolves made their dens, and wild game of every variety which existed in Michigan, was numerous and nearly unmolested? Where, oh where stood the original log cabin of the first pioneer? And where the old log hut of the hunter boys, and the spring of pure water. We were directed to a Mrs. Andrew Gleason, daughter of Nelson Chambers, whose handsome dwelling was a few rods distant. Making known to her our errand, Mrs. G. seeing her son ride into the yard in a buggy, took us at once to the high grounds, about eighty rods distant, where her father erected the first log house, and then to the grounds where stood our cabin. Mr. Chambers returned toward evening. As did the father, near fifty years before, so did the son, give us a hearty welcome, and history thus repeated itself. The night was passed in sleep, no owls or panther scream disturbed our quiet slumbers.

The morning dawned most beautiful. Mr. Chambers spent the entire day with his horse and buggy reviewing the grounds. We first visited his sister, about two miles distant, who was the only one living who was there in 1839. She was then about nine years old, and well did she remember the two young hunters, Cook & Rhodes. Many scenes were rehearsed and the interview with her was exceedingly interesting to the writer. Here we obtained a brief sketch of the Chambers family.

Nelson Chambers was a native of Litchfield, Conn., and was born Sept. 5, 1806. He was married to Miss Emily J. Shephard, of Vermont, Oct. 16, 1829. He moved to Ypsilanti where he carried on for some-time the grocery business with success. He undersigned for a drover for a large amount and was financially wrecked, disposing even of his bedding to pay the debt. In trading his home there he took a lot of wild land in Allegan county which he knew nothing about, never having seen it. It is now the northeast corner of the village. He sought it out. A guide from Yankee Springs accompanied and assisted him in erecting the log house. It was covered with boards. Here he moved in April, 1839, with his family, consisting of his wife, one son, named Marshal, and two daughters named Amanda J. and Emily. As soon as bark began to peel in the spring the board roof came off and was used for a floor and elm bark took its place. He afterwards had three more children: Currance Ann, Cornelia Alice and George Bennett. Marshal died April 15, 1858. Amanda married Wm. Heydenbeck, and lives on a farm in Layton, two miles from the hotel, and has five children. Emily died in 1883. Currance Ann married Andrew Gleason, in the village, and has one son. Cornelia Alice married G. Chase Goodwin and resides at Grand Rapids. George B. married Emily J. Hayward and he now keeps the Wayland Hotel. Nelson, the father, lost his wife, Oct. 12, 1865, aged 58 years, and he died October 3, 1877, aged 70 years and 8 days.

Leaving here, we revisited the old spring and drank from the same fountain. These waters have been analyzed and are pronounced very superior mineral springs, and we are informed people visit them from distant points and take home the water. (Perhaps it was these springs which caused our speedy recovery.) They are not improved as they should be. Eighty rods from here was the black ash swamp where the wolves were trapped and where the grape vines hung. The railroad occupies the grounds in the swamp where our wolf traps were set and a few tamaracks and stumps still remain vouching for our accurate description given in the first chapters, excepting distances were a little too far. There, too, is the same river winding its way, not through a forest but through fruitful fields. There, on its banks, is the very spot where two wolves, in pursuit of a buck, crossed the stream, leaped upon the bank, and fell dead. Away to the east still stands the old maple trees where the wigwams of the Indians were, and still further up the river old Saginaw had his camp.

There was one yet to visit, a descendant of the missionary, Mr. Selkirk, and thither we bent our course. It was three miles distant and we will not complain, for Mr. Chambers did not, of the mud and water his fine horse passed through. Arriving at his house, there appeared before us a man of small stature who was born and brought up among the Indians and knew well their language and character. He was about fifty years old. He claimed that Saginaw was an Ottowa chief. Here he was certainly mistaken for Noonday was the head chief of the Ottowa tribe. He informed us that the old chief, Saginaw , was finally killed by his son-in-law, Shoah-mish, by drawing a fire brand from the fire and striking him on the side of his head. There was a knot on the brand which crushed through his temple and caused instant death. Adaniram Judson, the interpreter, was married and had one son. One day he was out in the woods and near his home; on his attempting to get home an ulcer burst inside of him and he could go no further. His calling for help could not be heard. He crawled around to gather sticks for a fire, but could not do it. He was found frozen to death on a log. He was a great loss to both whites and Indians. Adaniram's brother was Pe-make-wan. Gosa had a wife named Quimee. He was uncle to Lydia who lived with him and was so much abused. Chin-a-bee-nell was a son of Saginaw. White Pigeon was big and fat. Tuck-a-main was a great leader. Missionary Selkirk died in 1877 at the age of 87 years and was buried on the banks of the beautiful lake near his residence. He was a man beloved by all. His whole life was devoted to ameliorating the condition of the human family and especially the Indian race.

Returning on a different road, we passed through a forest of 160 acres. Here the woodmen were engaged with axes and saws, clearing up the trees as of old. Nearing the village, we paused at the cemetery where many dead repose; close to the entrance are the graves of Mr. and Mrs. Chambers, the place being marked by elegant monuments. Fond recollections seemed to cluster around these monuments, recollections of the great hearts that seemed first to penetrate the wilderness and welcome all. To look back through the vista of time, the time when the wild beasts bounded here unharmed, and gaze upon the beautiful residences, the substantial business buildings, it seemed as if we were living in another world. There are now about seven hundred people in the village. The large union school house is a fine ornament; there are 158 pupils.

R.G. Smith, W.L. Heazitt and H.G. Spaulding keep dry goods and groceries.

The grocery keepers are D.T. Hersey, D.W.C. Shattuck and C.J. Branch.

Two hardware stores, E.S. Fitch and F.H. Beach.

One wagon and blacksmith shop, R.H. Olive.

Three drug stores, John Chapel & Son, John Graves, (postmaster,) and H.E. Hawkins.

An exchange bank Pickett, & Turner.

Two blacksmith shops, Wm. Stockdale and H.T. Stringham.

Boot and shoe store, S.S. Miles.

Meat market, Wharton & Yeakey.

Harness shop, P.H. & W.H. Schuch.

Two hotels, Geo. B. Chambers and S. Hollister.

Flouring mill, L.F. Wallbrecht.

Foundry, W.V. Hoyt.

Printing office, Wayland Globe, Geo. Mosher.

Livery stable and buss line, H.H. Kelley.

Buss line, S. Huntley.

Undertaker, Geo. H. Heuika.

Barber shop, Chas. Ward.

Four physicians, J. Graves, J. Turner, R.H. Rino and C.W. Andrews.

A lawyer, John Turner.

Two milliners, Mrs. Cynthia Slade, Mrs. M.E. Snell.

One feed and one flouring mill, and two sash mills, Clark & Hicks and Arthur Clark.

A Methodist and Disciple church.

Cheese factory, Isaac B. Smith.

Cider, sorgum and paint mill, Barnes & Sons.

Brick and stone mason, A. Gleason.

Jeweler, Frank Covell.

Photograph gallery, S. Filley.

Masonic lodge, 100 members. Odd Fellows lodge. The village board consists of E.S Fitch, President, Geo. Mosher, Recorder, Peter Ross, Marshal and six Aldermen.

Hard maple trees on both sides of all the streets, afford beautiful shade in the summer. Artesian wells are found in all parts of the village by sinking a pipe from 25 to 60 feet, throwing the crystal waters from ten to twenty feet high. All the inhabitants are getting these wells.

Such is the onward march of civilization. The poor, friendless Indians, having been robbed of their birthright, driven from their homes and the graves of their fathers, wronged and defrauded in every possible way by the white man, who can deny but there is some excuse for their cruelty to captives? Tecumseh was right when he delivered his speech to his warriors just previous to the battle of the Thames. He foresaw their destiny and his predictions have been fulfilled. An inferior race must yield to a superior, who will have no respect for rights. Another century will wipe out every vestige of the Indian race on the American continent and they will only be known in history.